Make Friends Instantly!

(When You're Shy)

The Art of Making Friends

How to Make Friends as Introvert, Communicate Effectively,
and Overcome Shyness and Social Anxiety

Katharina A. Macher

Table of Contents

Introduction

Many of us have felt limited in their desire and need to communicate with others by social anxiety or shyness. How many times have you wanted to open a conversation with a stranger on a train or in a bookstore, but you couldn't, because you feared being boring, being rejected, or simply looking out of place in your attempt to socialize? How many times have you wanted to approach a girl or a boy you found attractive, but something prevented you from being confident and acting on your impulse? You may not realize it, but many people are affected by shyness in various social or romantic contexts, even though in certain areas of their lives they are quite certain of their abilities (e.g. professionally they know they are qualified). Shyness is a rather wide-spread psychological phenomenon and the truth is some people are so deeply controlled by it, that they may avoid admitting it to themselves or to others. That's why you might think you are alone in your concerns, but this is not true.

Some people often rationalize their social anxiety in forms and thoughts that are slightly more acceptable to them. Have you ever heard some nerdy guy claiming he doesn't give a damn about socializing and meeting new people? Have you ever heard anyone bragging excessively they can break the ice with everyone and also seduce practically anybody? Both behaviors conceal deeper issues that are rooted in the same problem: social anxiety. However such people are maybe too proud, maybe too scared to admit (even to themselves) they suffer or have suffered from anxiety and they try to cover up their problem instead of actively working on improving their communications skills. Daphne de Maurier explains this widespread issue quite beautifully in one of her novels when she says "I wonder how many people there were in the world who suffered, and continued to suffer, because they could not break from their own web of shyness and reserve and in their blindness and folly built up a great distorted wall in front of them that hid the truth".

This book is going to help you explore the problems that arise from shyness or social anxiety in a detailed way. By going through its pages you will learn how to discover that seed of confidence inside of you so as to improve your communication with people. Although communication is a multilayered issue, the purpose of this book is helping you overcome your barriers and insecurity and thus connect with people better. It is not rote communication or "tricks" to sell what you don't have that this guide centers on. Such a book addresses issues of social communication from the core by focusing on the root of these problems. It teaches you how to master conversation and to gain confidence in many life situations and contexts. Moreover, it shows you how a very common and sometimes undervalued social phenomenon, small talk, can smooth your path to better communication skills and a more successful life.

Read on and discover how you can intelligently tear down the walls that your shyness often builds around you!

1 |
How to Get Rid of Social Anxiety and Shyness

In this chapter we will look into the causes of social anxiety and how shyness affects communication and keeps us from building bridges and connecting with others. Psychology often associates shyness with introversion. Even though there is a grain of truth to this correlation, it's not always a rule. It would be more simple if matters were that clear: all extroverts are confident and outgoing, while all introverts are affected by social anxiety. The explanation for this idea which is somewhat exaggerated is the fact that introverts focus their energy on their own mental processes rather than on the outside world. Thus it's understandable that they will more frequently be wrapped in their own thoughts or feelings. Additionally, introverts have a smaller circle of friends. However that may be merely because they don't get bored of their relationships so easily; instead of looking for new friends, they prefer connecting deeply with fewer people.

One often hears claims that introverts hate small talk, since they prefer deeper discussions. In reality it's not "small talk" that introverts dislike. It is superficial relationships that they would like to avoid. If we look closer into what exactly the so-called "small talk" means or could mean, we notice that it refers to a rather enjoyable, entertaining, and connective type of communication, especially when implying the incipient steps and stages of getting to know people.

Once we realize we can find confident introverts as well as socially anxious extroverts, we understand that the cause of shyness or impaired communication doesn't lie in such an inborn orientation, but derives largely from one's individual psychology. More often than not shyness stems from insecurity – a less than ideal confidence in oneself, in one's personality, and in one's own charm. In less fortunate cases shyness is a longer-lasting effect of painful rejection (during teenage or youth, for instance) or of some other traumatic experiences e.g. lack of sufficient love in one's family environment, imperfect financial conditions or health etc.

There are a series of scientific causes of social anxiety such as an imbalance in brain structure that affects fear response or a so-called "learned behavior" which runs back to one's family environment. If your parents were too controlling and harsh, you may have adopted an indirectly related reaction that is triggered automatically in social contexts. Similarly, if they were too protective and engulfing of your personality, you may feel anxious when you have to act independently and spontaneously.

How does social anxiety manifest itself? Is everyone suffering from this "disorder" even aware there's something that should and *can* be "healed" or changed? Most people who seriously struggle with anxiety are stuck on a mental script (with a strong emotional background) that makes them fear they will be judged by people around them regardless of what they say. Sometimes they even fear others will notice their own anxiety, which of course amplifies everything. Consequently such people often avoid getting into dynamic social contexts, being the center of attention, speaking out and communicating spontaneously, or meeting new people for fear they will be judged or rejected.

The bottom line is whatever its original cause is, social anxiety comes down to an insecurity about one's own value and ability to build connections with people in a spontaneous and authentic way.
"Why would they want to talk to me?";
"What could I tell them to make them interested in me?";
"Won't they think I'm desperate and needy if I approach them and initiate a conversation?";
"How could we connect along serious matters when we don't even know each other?";
"What if they find my first utterances silly and boring and they refuse to

continue a conversation with me?";
"How could I say something that catches their attention on the spot and makes them want to befriend me?"

All these are questions that run through the minds of many people who suffer from shyness. Such people are bound by their own anxiety in social situations and that has quite frequently messed with their deeper (and sometimes more hidden) desire to start conversations with people in a very naturally flowing and easy way.

Often people have ingrained patterns which dictate what they think communication should be like. With so many *should* verbs in their mind, how could they not feel pressured and anxious? When you think a conversation should develop along fixed lines, you are likely to stumble and fear you may make mistakes.
"How could I approach a guy I like, if I'm a woman?";
"I should seem incredibly controlled and competent during this job interview. I should only talk about professional matters in the most formal way possible.";
"One should never joke around with shop assistants, because they are just strangers.";
"People should think I'm perfect and unbeatable, I must not let any wrong word or move slip through my behavior."

In reality spontaneity, an open mind, and a penchant for free-flowing and authentic communication that people sometimes call "small talk" will bring you much farther in your social life. What people sometimes call "small talk" with a tinge of condescendence is actually your key to developing better and broader communication skills and thus having a more active social life as well as more fulfilling relationships.

2 |
How to Make Catching Small Talk with Anyone

Let's Shatter Some Preconceptions about Small Talk

In her book on *Small Talk* Joustine Coupland draws attention to the fact that people confuse small talk with "unimportant talk" and thus this type of social interaction via flexible and spontaneous communication has "gained" a pejorative meaning. Are you familiar with MBTI (Myers Briggs Type Indicator)? You probably are. At least you've come across this personality theory online, in school, while talking to your friends, of at work. Have you ever read type descriptions? "INTPs are extraordinarily clever and abstract and they hate small talk". Have you ever heard someone talk about their type on YouTube or among your friends? "I am INTJ, the mastermind, and I am bad at small talk". Sometimes a slight dichotomy between consistent/deep conversation and what is commonly called "small talk" is not even implied anymore; there are people who directly state and show their dislike of such a ways of connecting socially and their hostility towards it right in the middle of a conversation. They abruptly change the subject or they start scolding or mocking at their interlocutor once communication slips into "small talk".

The bottom line is understanding that small talk is actually your path away from shyness and lack of social confidence and into interesting and dynamic interpersonal relationships. Of course you shouldn't limit yourself to small talk; on the contrary, you are welcome to dive into elaborate topics (artistic, purely professionally, and even philosophical). The point is that small talk is a first step towards effective communication and an active social life. You won't get rid of insecurity or shyness by discussing politics and business only. It's much wiser to use small talk as your bridge towards deeper topics and relationships. Do you know how powerful the art of small talk can be during a job interview? If you can easily perform this kind of relaxed and natural communication, your chances of getting the job can be higher than those of another candidate who has more diplomas and experience. Naturally one doesn't substitute the other. Competence, expertise, and efficiency are still highly important. But mastering the art of small talk as well as conversational intelligence will increase your charisma, your connection with people beyond a purely formal context, and your chances to succeed.

So what *is* small talk after all?

- For starters, small talk is not necessarily talk about the weather, nail polish, football, Lady Gaga, or junk food. Small talk is not gossip. This type of conversation is actually much more spontaneous and all-encompassing than we think.

- Small talk does not necessarily imply fixed openers, a succession of greetings and standard replies, or highly predictable content. The real meaning of small talk is that of a social lubricant whose functionality is low. You don't do small talk to earn money. You don't engage in this kind of conversation to solve complicated problems. You generally avoid small talk when you have to undergo an examination at school or when you must seriously perform and complete engrossing tasks at work. Small talk is just something you enjoy for its own sake, even though you have no idea what it will lead to.

- Small talk does not require standardized social relationships and it is usually not limited to the parameters of a given relationship. On the contrary, small talk is your tool for forming, changing, and more than anything improving social relationships. It's a preconception that you shouldn't engage in small talk with your potential future boss or a person who ranks higher than you somehow. The key to effective small talk is intelligent and multifaceted communication that includes non-verbal language, rhetoric games and devices, subtle networks of allusions and meanings, and an authentic drive towards people. The last part of what great small talk is should actually come in the foreground, because otherwise you won't find it easy to get rid of social anxiety. Only a genuine interest in people will cure your shyness. But if you are reading this book, chances are you already have it in a high degree. You just need to find the right tools for compelling and constructive social communication.

- In language theory small talk is defined as phatic communication. Does that phrase scare you? "Oh, man, is that what small talk is actually about?" Should you learn such theoretical and scientifically juicy vocabulary in order to get rid of the thorn in your side, aka social anxiety? Terrible! Now you have to change all your notions about social communication and turn them upside down. Don't worry, this phrase was just meant to give you a glimpse into the broader importance of small talk. Phatic communication refers to an act that is not centered on conveying "hard" factual information. Its function is one of performing a social task. In other words, phatic communication is meant to smooth out social dynamics and help you connect with people you may or may not know.

- Small talk is amazingly versatile. When you just communicate for pleasure with people without any precise functionality, you can basically talk about anything you want. We all know that we give our best especially when there's no pressure like the sword of Damocles above our heads that we are going to be judged or that we'll lose something significant if we don't perform well.
Have you even gone to a job interview in a relaxed and casual mood and actually got the job not only because you fit the profile required and the corresponding competences, but also thanks to your conversations skills? There are people who happened to bump into their interviewer on the hall while they were getting their coffee before their job interview. Without having any clue about the identity of the person they came across, they started a casual warm conversation which actually urged their boss-to-be to offer them the job. They proved to be impressive, authentic, and "human" in their spontaneous social communication apart from competent.

That certainly tells us lots about people's personality that is often suppressed and concealed, if they think they have to be formal and rigid instead of their natural selves. When they go to a job interview, some people think the employer is looking for an abstract model instead of a real person. And they are wrong.

- Small talk should be regarded as a social space that has high energetic value and can be filled with a lot of content that may differ from one context to another. The point is that small talk is bound to help you connect with people. Thus it is a channel through which you transmit positive relational energy, which is much harder to accomplish when you have to perform functional talk that has a clearly defined purpose and implies time- or –benefit related conditioning. Small talk simply places you in the same setting with people and it is up to you to fill that "social room" with the energy of your choice. Of course, if you only talk about the gloomy weather or the way autumn left all the trees lonely and empty... you can't really expect people to love you, can you? That's why first and foremost you have to get rid of preconceptions about small talk. It is as good as you make it. There are hardly any rules for small talk. You can be as creative as you want with it. Small talk is actually something you can perfectly adapt to your social goals – not the other way round. If you desire to conquer a woman, you are going to use a particular approach. If you are waiting in a queue in your supermarket and you want to get in contact with the person in front of you, naturally you are going to rely on what's going on in that very setting or on what strikes you about their looks or their personality.

3 |
How to Become a Magnet for Friends

Now that we understood that small talk is by no means trivial or unpleasant, but a pool for social "mobility" that you can use to its full potential, let's see how you can actually enhance your communication with people and say goodbye to shyness.

Amazing Verbal Communication

- The rule of thumb when you try to connect with people is that compliments are golden. However you may want to be ingenious in your approach and not resort to crass flattery or lies. Compliments are actually much better treasured when they are a bit sparse or when they come from someone who is regularly inclined to be rather objective and critical. Have you ever had a boss who could make you feel you still have lots to improve, then give you a rise with or without any words? Have you ever had a teacher who would first show you how high your potential could be before praising you for your actual results? Compliments are priceless tools, but keep in mind that most people are actually intelligent and perceptive.

Concrete Openers and Lines to Help You Succeed

Small talk doesn't mean trying to trick an older man into believing he looks as if he were 20 years old or telling someone who has just had their hair cut that they look awesome when the style clearly doesn't suit them. Here are a few "tricks" that can do wonders:

> *"It struck me right from the first second I saw you - I bet everyone tell you that you look like Penelope Cruz, but I actually think your allure is much more mysterious and clever.";*
> *"I've always thought people in France mainly care about eating good cheese and drinking Bordeaux. How come you're so reflective and hardworking?"*

Of course, you should make sure any tinge of humor or irony are clear enough with such openers. You are only *referring to* stereotypes and using them as a bridge towards the other; you don't want to appear prejudiced or narrow-minded. The point is using much too direct, self-understood, and transparent compliments is not going to lead you anywhere. People are bored by clichés. They like it when others take them by surprise with a twist and even when they have to wonder a bit whether someone is serious or ironic. If you sense the person is quite self-confident, be a bit bolder:

> *"Your aquamarine hair stripes are definitely something! Did you actually order them or you got them for free as an experiment?"* or
> *"I saw the advertisement for Zara that used exactly your blouse. It's really cool. Honestly you look a bit like the model, but I wonder if you're not one size larger."*

Keep in mind such quasi-sarcastic and "punchy" openers may not be the right choice if you're dealing with a person who might actually feel insulted. In case you want to compliment a woman for her good looks while still saying something on-the-edge and not overly banal, you can use such lines.

Small talk must be genuine and flexible. Find something you really like about the person you want to communicate with. Make sure you compliment them in a clever way. Language is your secret weapon – you are the master of all its potential, not the other way round! Some people love it when they are complimented in a highly allusive or ambiguous way (and they are challenged to discover the real meaning behind words). Others respond better to a more provocative and maybe slightly ironic style, lest they may feel the other wants something from them instead of communicating spontaneously. Ideally you should be extremely perceptive and also a bit versatile in your small talk. Try to sense what works with certain people. Don't blunder by applying automatic techniques with people who may not actually like a specific approach. Just be totally present in your social context and let your intuition guide you!

- Practice your conversational intelligence when engaging in small talk. As you may know, there is not only one type of intelligence. Maybe your social anxiety is caused by a feeling that you are not exactly a genius. Maybe you fear someone may find what you say dull and uninteresting. Maybe you didn't get your dream job yet or some of your teachers made you feel uncomfortable, because they didn't consider you well-prepared enough for very high grades. Regardless of the cause of your shyness and implicit fear of failure, now it's time to learn that intelligence is a multifaceted and dynamic quality. Don't try to measure up to the wrong people while ignoring strengths you already have. You don't have to be Shakespeare, Lars von Trier, or Nikola Tesla in order to be smart and have people acknowledge your intelligence. As Howard Gardner explains in his theory of multiple intelligence, some of us are endowed with logical-mathematical smarts, others with linguistic, bodily-kinesthetic, spatial, musical, interpersonal, or intrapersonal intelligence. So as to get rid of social anxiety and make friends easily, you actually don't need to be Einstein or Goethe and produce smashing work that brings you broad social recognition. All of us have at least one type of intelligence. Small talk is based primarily on interpersonal and linguistic intelligence and the good news is that both can be easily practiced – and improved!

Judith Glaser wrote an intriguing book on what she considers to be conversational intelligence. She regards it as an art that can help us get our desired results in many life situations: at work, when we have to collaborate with others in a team, in our family relationships, in our romantic life etc. While it tangentially intersects with the essence of small talk, it is definitely a skill to develop in order to make your communication as fruitful as possible. Conversational intelligence is based on a clear perception of the interlocutor's perspective and mindset, on empathy or emotional awareness, on building trust, and on the ability to grasp assumptions and avoid preconceptions that may involuntarily affect our communication.

- Build rapport! What does this mean exactly? Please keep in mind some people misunderstand what real rapport and they use this term in a wrong way to refer to mirroring your interlocutor or pretending to be similar to someone in order to make them like you. In fact rapport implies actual communication and connection: listen to what your interlocutor says; ask other people many questions; pay attention to them as well without being totally self-absorbed; let yourself drawn in by their personality; find common ground that is based on deeper resonance and not just artificial things. Last, but not least, be completely present in a given communication setting and allow yourself to enter a dance of words and gestures that will bring you closer to people. Don't get stuck on what you think you should say or do, because real communication does not mean memorizing a few lines and learning technique. Rapport is primarily an emotionally-based kind of communication that you can perform by means of verbal tools.

So how can you actually build rapport with someone? Let's say you see a person in a supermarket who wants to buy a product, but they are not very sure it's the right choice. You are not actually interfering with their discretion or being intrusive if you drop a line or two about your experience with the same product:

> *"I understand your concern and I hesitated before purchasing that blender for the same reasons. Well, let me tell you I actually found it very satisfactory: great speed and power despite its not very high price. If you want my opinion, I recommend that you trust this brand. You don't have to buy something more expensive, it's really good!"*

Thus you are already drawing a fine connective line between you and the other person, as you've already experienced their doubt. Alternatively if you see someone displeased or bored in a bus station, you can easily use rapport make small talk while you both wait for your bus:

> *"I hear you, it happens kind of often ... I was also upset the bus was 20 minutes late last week. I hope you're not actually under lots of pressure, are you? Do you have to get anywhere at 13 pm sharp?"*

We're mainly talking simple and mundane situations here ...but that's the good start on the path to building rapport. Of course, if you have more time at hand or you're dealing with a more complicated situation, you can show sympathy or simply ask more questions to help the other person talk and get their burden off their chest. The notion that people you don't know are total strangers may be a bit delusive. We have similar experiences throughout our lives, we just don't know it or we may just use superficial signs and think we don't.

- Anchor your communication. How can you do this? The art of small talk start from its rather context-dependent nature. By no means is this a disadvantage, although you may be tempted to think it is. Refer to something the other's behavior or attitude that you have just seen and liked; make a clever joke out of an unpleasant situation (e.g. if you have to wait too long in a queue). If you have already started a conversation, ask them about their clothes brand while subtly complimenting them etc. You can even spontaneously start talking about a product you have just bought and ask someone you're interested in to share their opinion on it: *"Was it really worth the money?"; "Do you think this color suits me?"; "I wonder if I could find a better brand for the same kind of product somewhere ...".*
  The key to effective and practical small talk is avoiding rhetorical questions and offering the other person the opportunity to respond in a real manner. Show curiosity about their actual opinion and experiences, don't just throw 1-2 random questions out there as if you didn't even care about what they reply. Questions whose answer is self-evident *("It's kind of cold in this supermarket, isn't it?")* as well as cliché-ridden lines (*"You look like my ex girlfriend."*) should be avoided if you really want to make interesting small talk.

Ideally you should avoid anything negative or "gross". If you're dissatisfied with the effectiveness of a service or if a shop assistant seems unresponsive, starting to complain about that with another person in the shop is not the right way to do small talk. What you can do is twist that unpleasant situation into a "hook" for communication.

"Is there something about me that makes the shop assistant so passive and indifferent? Do you think my hat scares people away?" or "If, unlike me, you know the secret to making shop assistants hurry up to help you out ... please do divulge!"

The best way to start small talk and make friends instantly is to show genuine interest and even touch upon more "complex" matters, once in the middle of a conversation. For instance, if you are travelling and you see another tourist in a souvenirs shop, you can ask them a targeted question about a product you want to buy.

"What do you think is more representative of this culture? Have you already seen anything more interesting and catchy in a different place by any chance?"

After you have made your way into a conversation and if you like the person and want to go further, you can ask them about their opinion on that particular city or the country you're visiting:

"So what do you think Germans are really like? Do you agree with the usual stereotypes? Honestly people I've met so far are not really as dry and formal as some may say." or
"How have you enjoyed your stay in Copenhagen so far? Have you already seen the Nyhavn? Is it as impressive as in pictures"

If you are visiting a foreign place and you're on the verge of losing your way, of course you are going to ask for directions out of need. And yet you can come across someone you can take the conversation further with and you can do it in a funny way, acknowledging the other as a person in their own right:

"Do you think I'm going to starve in this corner of the city this night if I go that way?";
"You look so much like a textbook Italian! You're probably a local. Might I kindly ask you to let me know if there's any chance of finding any shop open somewhere until 9.30 am?"

Amazing Nonverbal Communication

- What is nonverbal communication? Some of us underestimate the importance of this dimension of communication. Picture that a whole new discipline in Communication Sciences was created when Philippe Turchet wrote his book on *Synergology*. This new discipline focuses exactly on non-verbal communication skills and on ways of interpreting as well as improving body language, gestures, eye contact, posture, and paraverbal language (intonation, pitch, tone etc.). Do you realize now how vital the nonverbal level is in your social interaction?

- Make plenty of eye contact! This is your path to getting rid of shyness. If you struggle with social anxiety, you probably usually avoid looking straight at the other or into their eyes for fear you may be judged. However it's essential to use good eye contact, especially when engaging in small talk, because it will help you gauge people's reactions as well as their likes and dislikes much better. Avoid too insistent or confrontational eye contact. Nonverbal communication doesn't have to be turned into a power struggle or an invasion of personal space. Use controlled and moderately intense eye contact for optimal communication. Don't stare, simply move your eyes freely to other people or objects around as well, and make "reassuring" eye contact frequently. The best eye contact has an open and pulsating quality: you take your gaze away during conversation; then you resume this nonverbal communication by making sure the other person is actively listening to you, they are interested in what you say, and are not in any way disturbed by the content of your conversation. Ideally you should make steady and warm eye contact. Remember that a shifty gaze can signal dishonesty, while simply looking down at your feet instead of at the interlocutor actually means you are not open, but you let your shyness and insecurity control you. Gazing up at the sky for no real reason suggests you may be too dreamy, detached, and "head in the clouds", which actually means you are not very interested in communicating with people. Eye contact can be practiced until you learn to base your social conversations on a direct, reliable, steady, and friendly kind of gaze.

- Body language is extraordinarily important in your communication. It's hard to get rid of anxiety if you don't regulate your body language. Keep your body (especially your spine) straight and avoid any kind of gestures that indicate you are closed off, barricaded inside your own space, bored, excessively aggressive, or distracted. If you are standing, avoid crossing your legs or keeping your hands in your pockets unless it's winter and you're totally freezing outside. Keep your shoulders straight and your arms relaxed. If you are sitting, don't cover your face with your hands and don't sprawl your legs. Keep a relaxed, but also elegant and dignified posture. Men may think the so-called "Alpha male" posture that implies occupying as much space as possible and spreading your legs and your arms is actually persuasive or seductive. It may be for some only if it comes naturally and you are not invading anyone's space just to look "grand and tough". You can have a confident posture that draws people into conversation without trying too hard to be dominant.

- Avoid covering your mouth with your hands or biting your lips. It's true that sometimes social anxiety may make us yield precisely to these gestures in an automatic way, if we try to do something with the tension we may feel. However we can really train our body language. Keep your mouth relaxed as you talk: avoid pursed or tight lips, as they can indicate lack of social openness, rigidity, or disapproval. Any kind of positive and open gestures are encouraged, while tense and aggressive moves must be kept in check. No clenched fist or arms tied together in a defensive posture. Wide open arms, your palms facing upwards, a relaxed and aware handshake that only suggests equality are your tools to improved communication. You are free to use emphatic gestures with your whole arms if they help you express real positive emotions such as joy, pleasant surprise, admiration, affection etc. However pay attention to personal space. If you are already friends with someone, you are free to hug them. If you are just getting to know people, keep a moderate and open social space. Use friendly and inviting gestures that could show you are confident, optimistic, and curious about the other person, but don't invade their own space. Similarly, avoid keeping too much distance, even though you may fear closeness. Try to create an implicit tangential space between you and the other that you can sometimes fill with warm and open gestures while also keeping an active "barometer" on how your interlocutor may perceive or may feel about that.

- One aspect that you can be highly permissive and creative with are facial expressions: the more, the better, especially if they are bright, warm, optimistic, interested, and affectionate. You can afford a provocative look, an expression full of irony, or a mischievous smile from time to time; avoid expressions that show skepticism, hostility, boredom, fear, stress etc. Make sure you don't get too dramatic and exhausting in your facial expressions. You can be dynamic and present in real-time communication and thus maintain an energetic level of activity via emotionality as well. What you have to be careful about is that your expressions actually match your words and there's no artificiality or exaggeration in what you do.

- Voice inflexions and intonation are also quite important, especially when you make small talk. Why? Because in a purely and heavily factual kind of interaction people's attention is likely to fall on the information that is being exchanged. During small talk the emotional or energetic level of communication is almost as significant – think "chemistry", if you wish. How you say something will highly influence the other person's opinion about your or their interest in continuing the conversation. Of course, it's hard to change the natural qualities of your voice. If your voice is rusty, you won't automatically get a high-pitch voice out of the blue. If your voice is highly feminine and silky, use that to your advantage! The point is to be as creative as you can with your voice and make generous use of paraverbal signals. Avoid keeping a monotonous, weak, dry voice or getting too loud, strident, and abrasive in your communication.

4 |
How to Build Self-Confidence. Let Your Ego Shine!

It is important that you realize small talk isn't necessarily about persuasion unless we're talking about convincing the other to go on interacting with you. Small talk is mostly a "feel-good" kind of communication that should help you connect with people. For this reason you have to stay as natural as possible. Trying to "force yourself" onto others or seeming too desperate to persuade them about your own qualities (in a straightforward way, that is) may actually work in your detriment. If you have high self-confidence and you make intelligent conversation, your personality will automatically attract people and you won't have to push any boundaries or to brag about how cool you are. Remember that Lao Tzu perfectly grasped the core of self-confidence and great interpersonal interaction in his wise words: "Because one believes in oneself, one doesn't try to convince others; because one is content with oneself, one doesn't need others' approval; because one accepts oneself, the whole world accepts him or her."

That said the path to being confident is having a strong ego. What exactly does that mean? We understand the notion of "ego" not as a far-fetched self-image here, but as a healthy form of self-esteem that is rooted in the belief in one's potential, a realistic, but decidedly positive self-image, and authentic self-love. It is essential to specify that a strong ego doesn't mean narcissism or arrogance. It is based on a healthy and justified sense of pride as well as on a balanced perception of oneself and others. People whose ego is really strong have both self-respect and respect for others. A strong ego doesn't mean treading on others or ignoring their values or needs.

How to Strengthen Your Ego if You Suffer from Social Anxiety

Here are a few tips:

- Focus on your positive qualities and don't linger on your failures. If you are prone to being self-critical, try training your own thought processes and don't get stuck on negative experiences anymore. Think about the happiest moments in your life, the people you love, and your strongest passions. Write down what actually shapes your sense of self, if you have to. What defines you? What distinguishes you from other people? What do you love most about yourself? What have other people told you they absolutely like about you? What are the qualities you look for in other people when you try to build relationships? What are the most amazing places you've seen and the most awesome things you've done in life? These are just a few basic questions that will help you clarify yourself to yourself, so to speak.

- Take on new hobbies, start learning a new language or playing a musical instrument; don't allow yourself to be stuck in routines only. Seek new experiences and people, participate to social events, attend parties, spend lots of time outdoors, enjoy nature. Anything new and "not trodden yet" by you will bring a sense of freshness and spark in your life. This will indirectly make your ego stronger, because you'll feel what you are doing is worth it and you are a complex and capable person.

- Stay fit and make sure you look good. By that we don't mean model looks. Enhance what you already have and let your inner beauty shine and make your outer one hard to resist! While looks are not everything, it would be a bit hypocritical to say that they don't matter at all. What are the most beautiful things about your appearance? Discover them and carry them proudly! Buy only clothes that totally suit your body type and your personality, stay trendy, and also remember to appreciate other people's beauty.

- Get rid of negative people who hold you down or by some other means don't encourage you to love yourself. Anyone too critical, too aggressive/controlling, evil, or excessively depressive and hateful should be "removed" from your life. The truth is some people had to cut off relationships with individuals they actually loved for such reasons. It may hurt, but your self-esteem is far more important.

- Stay realistic and only focus on what you can do. Try introspecting a lot in order to find out what is both suitable for you professionally and makes you happy at the same time. Avoid flying too high, lest you may burn your wings. Similarly, don't stick to jobs or places that don't fulfill you only for the sake of money, for instance.

- Don't dwell on negative experiences and don't proliferate negative emotions. If you happened to go through something less pleasant, pushing it under the carpet won't do much for you, either. Do you have a blog or a diary? Write about what made you suffer. Do it incognito, if you have to. Once you process those unfortunate experiences, you will feel free. Take the burden off your chest and your ego will shine (even though it may take a while).

- Don't let other people define you. You are the one who knows best who you are and what your strongest attributes are. Even if you experience something more challenging (e. g. you were rejected by someone you liked or you didn't get your dream job), keep your positive frame of mind and don't let someone else's feelings or perspective on you affect your sense of self.

- Try to get out of your comfort zones once in a while and seek challenges. Don't stick only to people you may consider to be "way bellow you" intellectually and do your best to learn something new on a regular basis. Try practicing a new skill or a new hobby; enroll in some new courses, if you're older; get in contact with people who can teach you things.

5 |
What Does It Take to Be Charismatic?

What is charisma? Is it something inborn? What skills or qualities does it imply? Charisma is a combination of unique people skills, high self-confidence, wit, insight into what makes other people tick, alert and versatile intelligence, and a compelling "vibe" (or overall energy) that others find contaminating. As you can see, charisma is a complex of a wide variety of factors in your personality. How could it only be a native endowment then? It implies strong verbal skills and the ability to communicate in a way that is both natural and persuasive. People who are charismatic can easily make friends or win followers. At the same time, they are entertaining and can make others really listen to what they say (e.g. they have lots of stories to tell). Charisma also means a strong ego and the ability to instantly "seduce" people and make them feel liked or acknowledged. Highly charismatic people know how to bond with others in a way that makes them feel they are also interesting. When a charismatic person pays attention to others, they already create an emotional undercurrent along with a conversation and that energy is positive, refreshing, and revitalizing. Being charismatic means being riveting in a fashion that can be sensed as you personal charm or distinguishing "mark". People are hardly ever charismatic in a totally abstract or unclear way. Usually it is easy to tell what is fascinating and interesting about them.

"All right. Wonderful!", you will think. "What can you do to *become* charismatic?"

How to Enhance Your Charisma

- Learn the art of giving compliments. Try to be as sincere and possible and avoid clichés. It's time you realized that complimenting people on all-too-obvious physical features or on qualities they actually don't have is not going to lead you anywhere. Usually people know when they have "bright green eyes", "nice hair", or "a trendy burgundy coat". Go deeper than that, spot what people may be slightly unsure about ... but choose something that is actually true! Don't get down to the level of unctuous lies. People are smarter than you think and they can't be tricked so easily. Find something that's not extremely visible or slightly "on the edge" e.g. a personality feature that may or may not be considered to be wonderful (*"You seem so temperamental and challenging!"*), a bona fide intellectual quality (*"You made a really great point here, because..."*), or an item that could seem strange, but perfectly fits their personality (*"I kept staring at your interesting jacket. Turquoise is certainly not everyone's color, but I have to say it totally complements your chill, urbane, and ethereal spirit."*). By giving the right compliments you show you actually acknowledge people and notice even the subtlest aspects of their personality. Charisma doesn't mean selfishness or self-absorption. It is the ability to perform authentic, enthralling, and multifaceted communication.

- Build a strong identity and make sure you know your values and your beliefs. When someone asks you your opinion on a certain matter (e.g. politics, religion, art etc.), always be ready to express your opinions and elaborate on them in a way that shows you have truly congruent and sophisticated convictions that you consider to be part of your overall personality. Charismatic people more often than not have distinct and quite strong opinions on many things in the world around them and they can convincingly explain them to others. Of course in order to be charismatic you have to stay tuned and acquire a lot of information on various topics such as literature, movies, fashion, culture, musical trends, social causes and so on. One can hardly be charismatic when one doesn't really give a damn about anything happening in the world and only talks about what they eat daily. If you find yourself in a waiting room and you'd like to talk to the person sitting next to you, you can simply ask them a question that anchors both of you in the city life: e.g.

"Have you perhaps been to ____ (insert film or music festival here) this year? I missed it because I had to travelled, but it would be cool to hear some opinions on it." Or

"Do you think ____ (insert artist/film here) really deserved winning that award the other day? Personally I found it/them kind of unconvincing ...could it be just me?"

Afterwards you can take it from there and dive into a more sophisticated conversation, if you want to.

You are not going to make small talk and befriend people instantly if you start talking about your opinions about homosexuality or pro-life causes. However you can make a sharp witty comment once you have already started a conversation with someone. For instance, if you have to wait in a railways station for a while and you want to start a conversation with someone next to you, you can say:

"Wonderful, my train will be 20 minutes late. That's exactly what I needed to boost my mood after the lousy creepy film I watched last night!".

Such a line is a perfect conversation opener in a spontaneous and promising way. Chances are your neighbor is going to ask you what movie it was and why it was so bad. So here you are: now you can turn your small talk into something more prolific. Remember: small talk is not empty or silly talk.

- Charisma is great to support if you have your own words of wisdom from what you read or watched on TV. Maybe you don't remember full quotes to the letter, but it's enough if you recall the main idea. Use others' thoughts and opinions to build a multilayered web of interpersonal communication. When you relate to something an author or a celebrity said, you are already building an abstract bridge between you and another personality. Take your interlocutor with you into such a network of ideas! Don't only stick to your own opinions and experiences; make many connections and you will increase the level of complexity of your communication along with your charisma.

- Humor, wit, and even the ability to be ironic or sarcastic (at least sometimes) are constituent parts of someone's charisma. Do you have your own arsenal of jokes and stories? Some people do in a natural, non-deliberate way and that makes them highly entertaining. Even if you don't, always be open to cracking jokes on the spot. Pay attention to funny sides of the situation you are in and use people's words as a "trampoline" for humor. What if someone may be sad or bored? If *you* are witty and lively enough through your communication style, your interlocutor will naturally be caught in the game and you will have an amazing control of the positive vibe in a conversation. Let's say you are on a train sitting next to someone who looks bored. You can open a conversation by telling a joke or being ironic and then stimulating them to tell you a story. For instance, unless you see a really hostile person, you can ask:
  "Is there something in the 1st class air that you dislike or are you travelling on a discount ticket?"
  If they answer in a bland voice and tell you that's just their mood, you can go further and ask them more: why? since when? anyone responsible? Make them open up to you. You can even more creative and start a conversation by asking for their input on a seemingly trivial matter:
  "I've just got a message from a friend who invited me to a costume party. Take a look at me and tell me: what do you think I should dress up like?"
  Of course such a thing could or could not be true, but it is probably going to be weird and quirky enough to attract the other at least into a funny retort, if not into a whole conversation.

- Cultivate a tinge a mystery and be ambiguous when the situation calls for it. Don't spill out everything that may cross your mind. People like allusive and subtle conversations whose meanings can be a bit of a challenge for them. Use banter, be slightly flirtatious, don't stick only to the formal and the literal!

- Be passionate about something … anything! And talk about your passion. Charisma implies a contaminating energy that can keep people amazed and full of admiration more often than not. If you talk about something that captivates you and makes your face light up and your voice vibrate with passion or enthusiasm, other people will automatically be held "captive" in your vibe as well as in the actual content of what you are saying. Do you remember that Robert Greene considered the Charismatic to be a distinctive type of "seducer" in his well-knows book *The Art of Seduction*? The allure of this kind of personality is in his view also based on the ability to be inspiring and stir strong emotions (even if slightly conflicting...). Charisma is high energy that emanates from you towards the other and that can usually happen if you talk about things you are passionate about and you believe in yourself.

6 |
When and Where to Connect with New People? How?

How to Initiate a Conversation

There's hardly any social context where a few people are brought together which doesn't allow you to make small talk and instant friends. Of course you may want to be more careful about delicate situations or places. If you are in a church, in the hospital, or in court for some reason, it's wiser to be a bit more reserved and precautious. However even in such places you could find someone you want to connect with and, if you are on the same wavelength and under fairly neutral to positive circumstances, you are free to make your small talk and get to know the other person.

For instance, start a conversation with someone who's in the same waiting room in the hospital, but avoid dwelling on negative issues. This way you'll distract the attention of both of you from more troubling matters and you'll enhance your mood. Ask them what they plan to do when they leave the hospital. Talk about the doctor. If you are totally annoyed you have to wait for hours in a row, start talking about some film you have seen. A few tips for good openers:

"Is this your first time in this hospital? What do you think about the personnel, are you satisfied with everything?";
"This waiting room and the atmosphere here remind me of a scene in Girl, Interrupted." (or insert another book / film you may know).;
"Wow, I'm not going to get bored now that I see this Cosmopolitan magazine here! I noticed you've already browsed through it. Have you found anything worthy of attention?" etc.

There's no better opportunity to get rid of your shyness if you simply start conversations with strangers in random places. That's especially true when your (potential) interaction will not affect you in any way and you can be as natural and spontaneous as you want. When you are in a public institution where you have to solve a problem, obviously small talk may affect your results. Or at least it might make people think you're not well-suited. You should be precautious if you want to make small talk right with the personnel at the embassy when you want to get your visa or in class with your own teachers.

Nevertheless in any totally neutral social context, you are quite free to tread on your anxiety and make small talk with people you find interesting. If you are at the dentist's, don't treat your doctor as a "professional" only. We are all humans and, if you notice the person is quite open to communication, go ahead. What could you ask your dentist, for instance? Just a few ideas:

"Where did you study Medicine? Do you have patients from all parts of the city? Do you think the equipment in Germany is much better than what one can find in the US?" and so on.

You can make small talk with the shop assistant in any kind of shop. Of course the conversation is not likely to be very long, but you *will* get rid of shyness and get in contact with new people! You have absolutely nothing to lose in such a context. Ask the shop assistant to give you advice on which color suits you better or ask them to show you where a certain kind of product can be found, how it works, and what you should choose for a given purpose.

"I love these trousers, but they're a bit large for me. Since you said it's the smallest size, do you think they'd look good if I ask a tailor to adjust them afterwards?";
"I'm going to purchase this suit and I'm interested in your personal opinion. What kind of shirt do you suggest I should wear it with?"

Of course oftentimes small talk is going to have a functional slant to in a shop. However let's be honest: sometimes you could really decide for yourself, if you had to, especially if you're an adult. Sometimes you just like chatting with others around you. You can also try to be a bit more "punchy" and add extra flavor to your interaction:

> *"I see you enjoy working in this outlet. I wonder... how many of your clothes are produced by this brand?"* or
> *"You strongly remind me of an actress I saw last summer in a play by Ibsen... are by any chance her or do you have anything to do with her? Have you radically changed your job?"*

Obviously some openers can be clearly only about phatic communication, namely gratuitous lines that have no real functionality. Take it as a game – the person you approach will probably realize when you're just coming up with something funny out of curiosity. They can respond in good humor or simply monosyllabically. If they enjoy it and play your tune, you win!

When you're in a shop or in a restaurant waiting for your food and you see someone you like doing the same, don't lower your stare or play games on your phone. Ask them something. If you want to be flirtatious and bold, try the following openers:

> *"It's the third time I see you having lunch in this Thai restaurant at 1 pm. I might think you're coming just to see me again!"*

Compliment someone standing next to you in the queue on their hair color or their trendy purse. If you're in a café, ask your neighbor how they discovered the place and what they like most about it.

> *"One thing I'd change is music ... why do they play Spanish guitar so often? Good Lord, it's so melancholy and gut-wrenching. Can you stand it?"*

Of course ideally you should discover more topics to touch upon after you address a person. However small talk can sometimes be done gratuitously, only because you are confident, you love interacting with people, and you literally don't give a damn about anything that could hold you back.

In a situation with more potential for communication e.g. in a bookstore, you can obviously go deeper. Let's say you see a person looking through a book by Günter Grass who is a bit undecided: should they buy it or not? If you're already familiar with the author, you can inquire why they hesitate and offer to help:

"Well, I've just seen you're a bit skeptical. Might I ask you why?";
"He's one of my favorite writers. Have you read anything his so far?";
"Didn't you like it or what else makes you skeptical?";
"Do you wonder which his best book is perhaps?"

Of course, you could be a bit wrong in your assumptions as you just start approaching the person (understandable!), but you will spark a conversation. They might reply that they don't know that author at all and are only looking for a gift. Well, that's the perfect opportunity to offer your useful opinion on the matter.

How about making small talk at work? While it is not always recommended to make small talk with your (future) boss, you should first of all gauge their personality. If you see your boss is communicative and curious about you, be brave and go ahead.

"Where do you have the strange paining on your wall from?";
"Who is the painter?";
"Is surrealism your favorite artistic movement?"

Go even further and ask them why they chose precisely that picture and what they like about it. If you see a photo of their family on their desk, don't hesitate – people usually love talking about their families. Ask them how old their daughter is and let them know if she takes after them.

"Does she plan to follow her father's career path and become a lawyer as well?" or
"Is this photo very recent? You seem to have a totally different persona right now. Did you work in a radically different niche?"

Be careful not to go too far in your inquiry. For instance, the last one is a line you should use for small talk with your boss only after you've already opened such lighter conversations. Otherwise it may look abrupt and out of place. In more relaxed and positively-charged situations, you can go as far as asking your boss what impelled them to choose that profession:

"Did you know this was your calling since you were extremely young? What or who inspired you on this path?"

This way you will get deeper into communication and your curiosity will show authentic interest in their own personality, not only in the tasks at hand or your strictly professional relationship.

There are myriad places where you can start communicating with strangers just for the hell of it – why not? People can be so fascinating! Many of them have hidden seas of stories inside them. We sometimes trivialize and mechanizise our lives excessively. If you are on a train, start a conversation with the person sitting next to you:

> *"What made you grab precisely a poetry collection for this ride? I don't know if I could stand poetry on the road.";*
> *„Where did you buy the book from? Have you read anything else by that author? Why would you recommend me to check his/her books out?";*
> *"Where do you live? Do you often make such trips?";*
> *"Are you generally satisfied with the railway service? Have they tried ordering any food ...is it worth it?" etc.*

One aspect you should pay attention to are the unwritten rules of personal space in public which may differ a bit from one culture to another. What may be quite frequent (and even annoying!) in Italy is likely going to seem a bit far-fetched in a country such as Germany or England. Make sure you are quite familiar with a few social habits of the people living in a place you're visiting so as not to blunder and make folks uncomfortable with your communication.

When you are standing in a tram station waiting for the vehicle that's supposed to take you home, don't ignore the people around you and don't look through them only. Look *at* or *inside* them. Ask them if that's their routine track or only if they're waiting for long and how they managed not getting bored. Say something amusing, but make sure you anchor your communication. Otherwise you may seem a bit weird and people might retreat in their shell. Avoid any "problematic" or "too serious" topics (e.g. money, marital status etc.). Make a joke that can lead to a short conversation:

> *"I think I saw you standing here one hour ago. Have you been waiting for the right tram since then?"* or
> *"Sometimes I think British people should be more chill and bohemian in means of transport. Why not get in the underground train with a bottle of vodka in one hand and a book in the other, as some Russians do? What do you think? Are you up to it?"*

If you like someone's coat a lot, ask them if they could kindly tell you where they purchased it from and when... perhaps you could find something similar. There's hardly any social situation that you cannot use to make small talk with people you want to get to know.

Of course, if you are romantically interested in someone, you can try a more provocative and courageous approach. But first and foremost do "test the water", otherwise they might find it strange you want to start a conversation. If non-verbal language tells you they may be also interested in you, take the first step! Don't just sit or stand there thinking about the person or glancing at them without saying anything out of shyness. In a potentially romantic context when you have some signs the person is not hostile, you can try much more banter, of course. Say something challenging e.g.

> *"Interesting coat! Is it a gift from your boyfriend?"* or
> *"Strange as it may seem, when I tried to find a real image for the character Daisy in The Great Gatsby, I used to picture someone similar to you. I wonder why."*

Of course the other person is likely to answer in a challenging or ironic fashion, but who cares? You have already started your conversation and you don't really give a damn about anything else – you'll find something smart to say to go on!

Keeping in Touch

What if you don't only want to befriend people in a blink of an eye (or through 1-2 well-laced witty utterances)? What if you'd like to actually keep in touch with someone you meet on a train or in a restaurant and literally become friends? Isn't it a bit "creepy" if you ask for their phone number? Especially if you're dealing with a member of your opposite sex (no matter what your actual sexual orientation is), you are probably going to come across a few preconceptions regarding such an act. However you can offer the person your credit card, your FB name, or your e-mail address. Personally I've experiences such stories. For instance, I did stay in touch with a lady I met on a plane. Honestly I was more self-absorbed and tired than her when we met at the airport. She approached me in the waiting room and I did respond to her first lines, but later I was a bit confused and exhausted by her need to chat all flight long. And yet we exchanged phone numbers and to my surprise she called me for Easter to wish me the best. I didn't instantly recognize her. She had to tell me who she was and mention something we talked about. But afterwards we had such a nice conversation! It was actually more pleasant and spontaneous than the one during our flight, because it was so gratuitous and it arose out of pure need, not boredom in a waiting room. We live in different cities, but we still keep in touch on FB and it's nice to know I met someone who remembered me and actually wanted to continue our relationship. So you see? Small talk can lead to beautiful results whether you plan it or not.

If you want to stay in touch, you could actually mention an event you're attending in the near future and invite the person you met to join you.

> *"You know, there's a cool exhibition in an intimate and modern gallery next week and I haven't talked to any other friend yet. If you'd like to join me, here's my e-mail address. Feel free to contact me!"* or
> *"I'm happy I met you and it would be awesome if we didn't lose sight of each other. You know what? I'm throwing a party in 10 days … it's my birthday. Please join, if you're up to it. I'll give you my FB info and add you as a friend. I will create an event anyway and invite you to let you know the exact time and place."*

There are many other possibilities to stay friends with someone you've just met. You can also be extremely spontaneous and come up with an idea *ad hoc*. Invite them to grab a sandwich after you meet, then exchange phone numbers. Come up with a few "tricks" for a project you could start together*:*

> *"Hey, listen, what a nice coincidence to have met you. I'm just starting up a project for translation services and I was looking for someone really good to help me out with Italian and French. Since you study these languages, would you be up to it?"*

Of course, it should be something doable and realistic. Your new friend might actually be interested!

Six Magic Words that Make Friendships Happen

Remember, it's not only what we say that attracts friends, it's how we act. Think about how you like to be treated, then offer the same (or better!) treatment to the people. There are **six magic words** that make wonderful, true and life long friendships happen. The six words are:

> *"What can I do for you?"*

7 |
How to Deal with Grouches

What should you do when you come across someone who proves to be a grouch? Well, sometimes you can misjudge people at first sight, it's kind of natural. The key is to hope for the best while also being prepared for the worst – with the right retort or comeback, that is. If you think the person is just being bored or uninterested, lighten up the situation and exit. They might answer only a "Yes" or a "No" and thus signal they're not up to more talk. That's one of the best scenarios following the one which actually gets you in real contact with people. You might bump into someone who only seems friendly, but is actually a narcissist or a bit of a jerk. They could hint that you should "get lost" or they could even utter insulting words. Your solution: never take it to heart! It's just small talk, remember? You're not actually losing anything. So what if one person wasn't interested in chatting with you? There are plenty of fish in the sea, as we all know.

Anyway you should probably not just bow your head and leave if someone is rude when you try to initiate small talk. You can be ironic or just find a humorous comeback. Don't be offensive, because you show you are quite affected and you don't take things as lightly as you seemed to (aka you're not totally confident). It can happen that someone you approached is brutal and rude when you ask for simple directions as a tourist, for instance. Personally I experienced this kind of negative turns:

"It's not my job to tell you what the right way is. I'm a florist, not a tour guide!" or *"Sorry, but I don't want to be bothered with such stuff!"* How should you respond in such a case? You have a couple of possibilities:

> *"Oh, mea culpa, I didn't know I'd meet precisely Queen Elizabeth II on this street! / "I've always thought Angela Merkel looks a bit different, but obviously there was some confusion in my head. I'm sorry if I disturbed you, Chancellor."* or
> *"Sorry, you must be leading a rather hard life, Ma'am. Would you like me to buy one bunch of roses from your shop for the price of four as a proof of my regret?"*

You could, of course, also try to appease the grumpy person you bumped into with something warm and funny, but chances are if they treated you badly, they won't actually give in to your small talk. That's why it's wiser to just give up on your attempt and make your exit. Let's say you asked someone in a shop to tell you where they bought their amazing posh purse from and they only answer in a condescending tone that it's none of your business. What should you say? Well, of course you could just utter something relatively humble and neutral:

> *"I didn't know my genuine curiosity would bother you that much. Enjoy your secret fashion code!"*

Alternatively you can swiftly shift the frame and challenge the person:

> *"Damn, Miss, how on earth did you realize I was a paparazzo prying for info to make a living out of your private life?!".*

If you don't mind turning your whole attempt at small talk into a battle of wits, you can go even farther:

> *"Really! Why not? If it were a hot quality brand, you'd have no reason to keep it a secret. Sorry I overestimated you."* or
> *"You're right, it's none of my business. But I was actually asking that on behalf of my boss, Professor Herbert. Please take this credit card and call us, if you're interested in having a book written about such an awesome person like you."*

In some cases you may be dealing with someone who's just a bit prejudiced about starting small talk or distrustful of strangers. If they are an open and clever person (and you don't actually want to communicate with narrow-minded people), they might actually laugh at your humorous comebacks and start chatting with you.

However don't turn that into your little small talk illusion. Pay attention to their words and their body language. If there's no sign of interest and openness, don't hope for a change of tide. Just show them you don't actually give a heck about their rudeness and hostility. No grouch will make you dislike small talk. You will certainly meet someone else who will enjoy interacting with you and you'll soon forget the rest.

Conclusion

This book was meant to help you work through your shyness and find effective and enjoyable ways to communicate with people and make friends instantly. It showed you that you are not the only one who has experienced social anxiety. There are also many people who managed to combat this problem by means of practice. This book was your guide to learning how you can practice both the right mindset for communicating with people in the most natural and positive way possible and the tools to using small talk as your bridge to getting to know new people. If you make small talk part of your regular activities and you engage it with a curious mind and an open heart whenever you have the chance, you will see your overall communication abilities will improve. Consequently, in more complex situations (e.g. your professional life, more serious romantic contexts etc.), you will have much more confidence and more skills to succeed.

Regardless of your age, gender, or culture, this book helps you take the first steps on the path to increased charisma, a dynamic social life, and more interesting and successful relationships, in general. Of course you can be as imaginative and creative as you want with small talk – there are hardly any rules and boundaries to it! Remember that some people look down on this kind of communication, because they think it is only about standardized empty language. They mistakenly think it's only something people resort to when they are bored on a train or when they have to greet their neighbor - while they actually don't give a damn about the person or the interaction. The truth is small talk is such a versatile tool precisely thanks to its gratuitous and spontaneous nature. There is nothing to lose... only things to gain: friends, experience, positive energy, information, and many, many others. So what you if you feel insecure or worried about how other people may react? Who cares? Start from scratch. Start with simple, everyday situations where it doesn't really matter where the conversation goes. Small talk is your tool for a more successful and enjoyable life as well as your weapon against social anxiety.

Start not giving a hoot about your shyness anymore and embark on small talk **with one of the first 3 people you'll meet** right after you've finished reading this book. You will see you will have already mastered a few things about the art of light, spontaneous, and genuine communication!

Yours sincerely,
Katharina

Getting Over a Breakup - Now!

11 Steps for Turning Your Worst Breakup into Your Greatest Opportunity

The Smart Breakup Recovery Guide

Have you recently gone through a tough breakup? Are you currently in the middle of a messy breakup and don't know how to break past this painful, negative cycle? Do you feel lost, alone, or powerless to survive this pain? If so, this book will help you finally get through the healing process quicker.

The healing process begins from the moment the breakup happens. With this book, you'll be able to take all the right steps to make sure that each day that passes is one day closer to full recovery. You will get through this and you will be stronger for it in the end.

In this book, you will find:

• Fast-acting strategies for dealing with the symptoms of heartache
• Release from the burden of hurtful memories
• The answer to why rejection is not about you
• Clear explanations about the underlying processes of heartache
• Motivation to keep pushing forward, no matter how hard the struggle is
• A comprehensive step by step guide to each of the 11 steps that will help you get through the healing process quickly
• Strategies for how to heal old wounds and free yourself forever

So if you are struggling with a painful breakup and feel completely lost and helpless, then this is exactly the book you need to help you realize your own strength and overcome this pain to become even stronger than you were before!

Available on Amazon:
ISBN-13: 978-1507805039
ISBN-10: 1507805039

Healing: How to Move Beyond Pain

Lift the burden from the soul and get over the pain caused by others

In this book you will discover how to improve your life by getting rid of any kind of pain that may be holding you down.

If you are going through a major breakup or you just experienced a disappointment that shook your belief system or your faith in yourself, you are certainly looking for means of breaking free from grief. You reached the right place!

In this book, you will learn:

- Understanding That It Is Not Your Fault
- How to Release the Burden of Hurtful Memories
- How to Forgive
- How to Let Go of the Past – Completely!
- Trusting Again
- Moving On in 6 Steps
- Practical Advice on How to Start Being Happy

This book was written to give you real information and real strategies for finding your inner strength and working through this pain to speed up the healing process drastically and unleash the best possible version of you.

Don't treasure your pain more than your own self. Start reading this book right away and effect the change you need in your life!

ISBN-13: 978-1514344026
ISBN-10: 1514344025

Disclaimer

Neither the publisher nor the author disengaged in rendering professional advice or services to the individual reader. Neither the author nor the publisher shall be liable or responsible for any loss or damage allegedly arising from any information or suggestion in this book.

Mention of specific companies, organizations or authorities in this book does not imply endorsement by the publisher, nor does mention of specific companies, organizations, or authorities imply that they endorse the book. Further, the publisher does not have any control over and does not assume any responsibility for author or third-party websites or their content.

Copyright & Legal Information

10228839R00027

Printed in Germany
by Amazon Distribution
GmbH, Leipzig